D0180227

# stuff on my cat

PRESENTS:

# WET CATS

BY MARIO GARZA

**CHRONICLE BOOKS**
SAN FRANCISCO

Copyright © 2008 Mario Garza. All rights reserved.
No part of this book may be reproduced in any form
without written permission from the publisher.

Library of Congress Cataloging-in-Publication Data available

ISBN: 978-0-8118-6227-1

Manufactured in China
Designed by Michael Morris
Illustrations by Deth P. Sun

10 9 8 7 6 5 4 3 2 1

Chronicle Books LLC
680 Second Street
San Francisco, California 94107
www.chroniclebooks.com

# INTRODUCTION

In the summer of 2005, I launched a Web site called Stuffonmycat. com. It began with a handful of photos of my cat, Love, covered in quarters, pens, bottle caps, keys, shoes, wallets, cameras, cell phones, and other miscellaneous things. I decided to ask others to join in on the fun; within a matter of weeks, I couldn't keep up with the thousands of submissions. Somewhere along the road, I received a couple of photographs of wet cats, and I chuckled—a lot. I couldn't help but remember the first time I gave a cat a bath. . . .

When I was about ten years old, our family took a weeklong trip out of the country. We came back during the hottest week of summer. As we were unloading our bags from the trip, some wild creature came waddling from the bushes toward us. It looked like a cross between an opossum and a small stray dog. It got a little closer, then it meowed an all too familiar meow. It was our cat Love, and she was completely covered in mud. What had once been the fluffiest cat on the block had become a brown, miserable rat-thing. She must have been having a high-flying backyard adventure, lost her grip, and fell into a puddle. Her meow expressed relief that we were finally home, though it was coupled with an evil glare, as if to say, "You go out of town for a few days and look what happens. Thanks a lot." She clearly held us responsible for her predicament. Her attitude toward us wasn't about to get a whole lot better, because it was bath time.

This would be Love's first bath. Like most cats, she absolutely hates water. We didn't know exactly how she would react to being given a bath, but we figured it would either be bad or really bad. So if this thing was going to be a success, we had to mentally prepare ourselves and come up with a game plan. What should have been a one- or two-person exercise turned into a family affair. Everyone had a job, and important tools to complete that job.

Escape guard? Check. (Dad) Scrubber? Check. (Mom) Towel operator? Check. (Sister) Cameraman? Check. (Me) Tube socks as arm protectors? Check.

Yes, my dad was more than prepared. If Love were going to claw his arms to bits, she'd have to go through an old pair of gym socks first. Our arsenal of goods in place, we moved to engage the enemy. Despite being on the opposite side of the house, Love knew that we had been plotting against her. We managed to corner her in the hallway: enemy captured. When she saw the tub of water and every single family member huddled in the bathroom, she knew what she was in for.

Once she was officially in the tub (never underestimate the power of hind-leg scratches), things started to calm down a bit. She realized there wasn't a great deal she could do, but she still fought. We struggled to wash the mud away, and she slowly became recognizable again. She had gone from fluffy calico to mangy brown rat to mangy calico rat—she still had to dry off. A few hours of toweling later, we had our old cat back, albeit slightly less trusting of humans. Her coat was shinier than ever, and she looked ten cat-years younger. As much as she had loathed the experience, I like to think that she was pretty pleased with her new appearance. I arguably had the best time throughout the whole ordeal. Not only did I remain relatively dry, but I also managed to capture some pretty hilarious shots.

The photo opportunities that pop up while bathing a cat are priceless, as you're about to see for yourself. We've gathered the best photographs of wet cats from Stuffonmycat.com to create this very special book. Most of the images are of cats having a bath (before and after); some pictures are of cats after they fell into a puddle or were caught outside during a rainstorm. Regardless of how these lovable felines may have gotten soaked, I think you'll agree that the results are hilarious.

—Mario Garza

!!!

HUNTER

# ASHTRAY

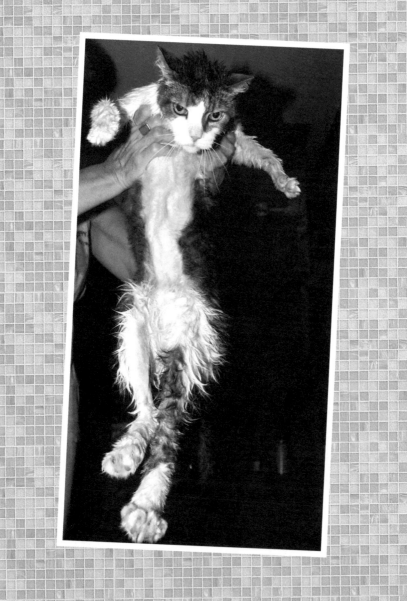

DRY CAT

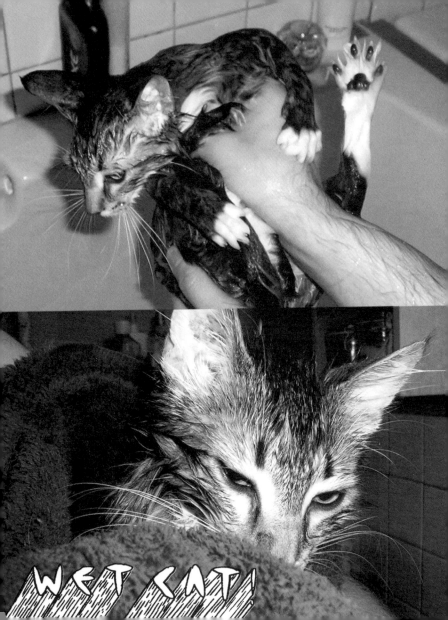

WET CAT!

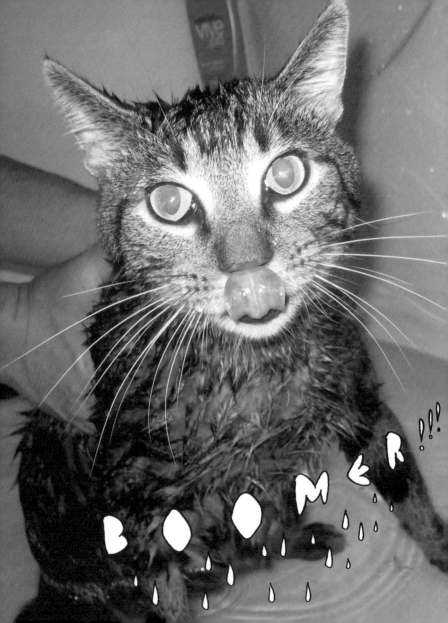

TWEEK

# DRY CAT

WET CAT!

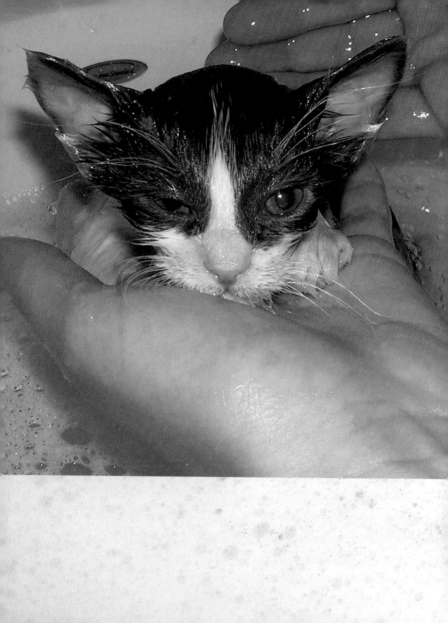

DRY CAT!

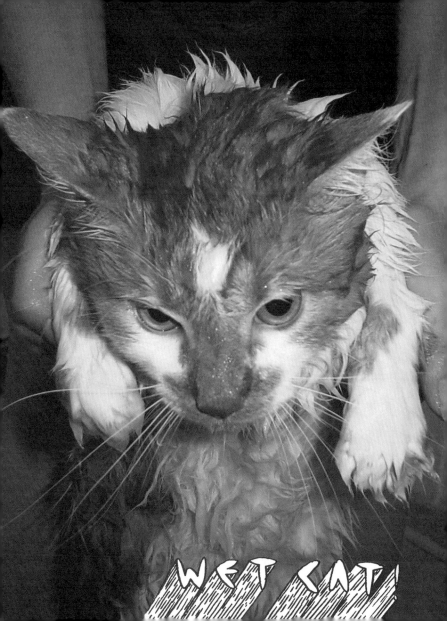

WET CAT!

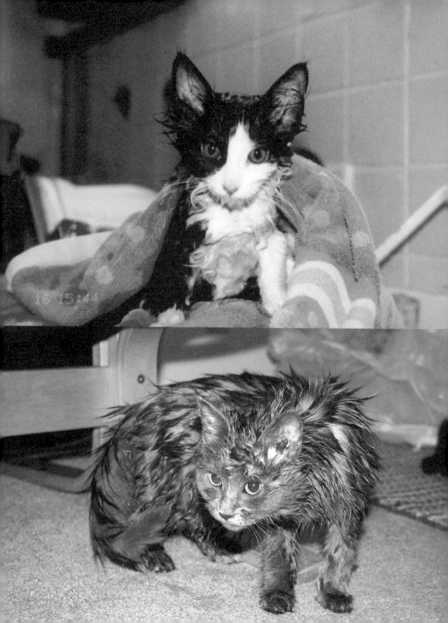

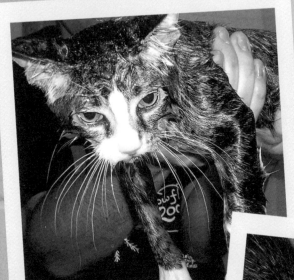

OREO

Cleopatra

DIESEL

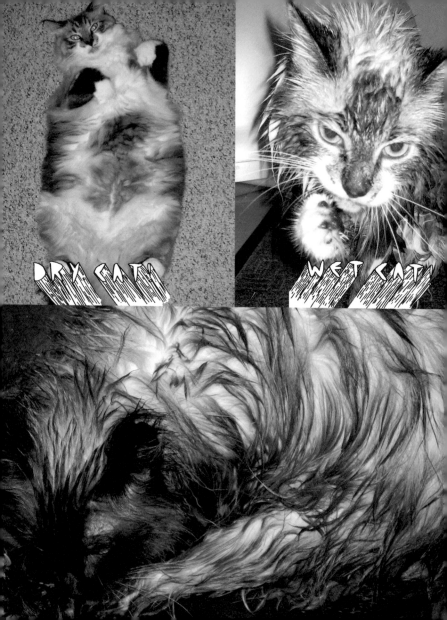

DRY CAT!

WET CAT!

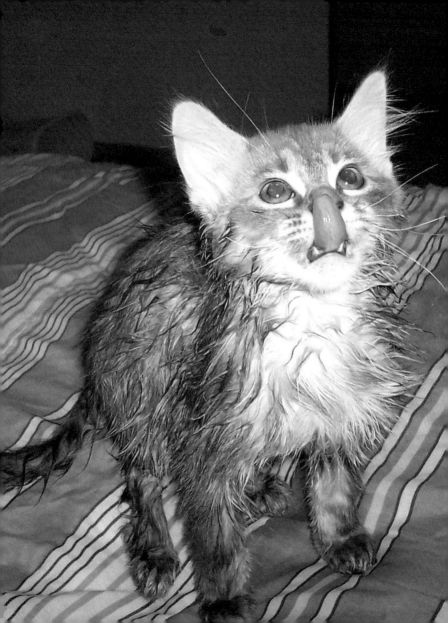

FLEURY

GRACIE

DRY CAT!

WET CAT!

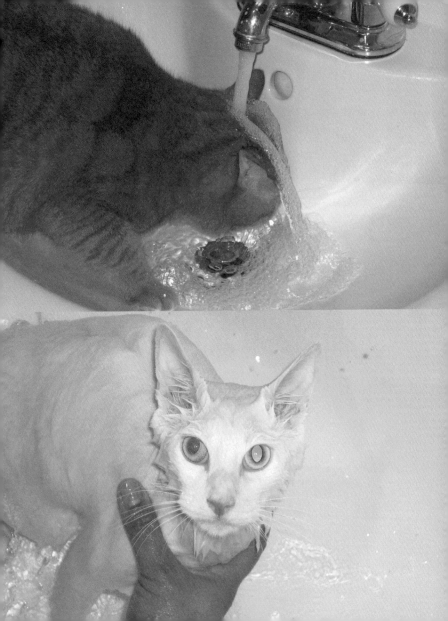

DRY CAT!

WET CAT!

IZZY

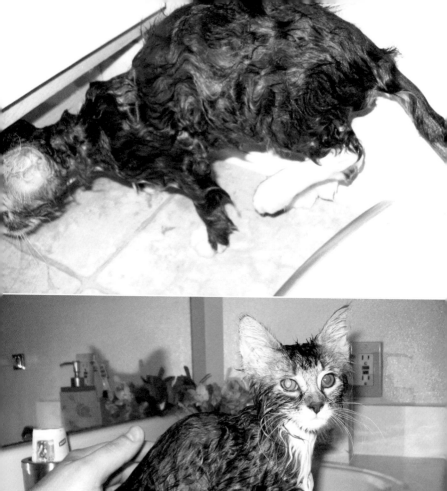

KITTIE PIES

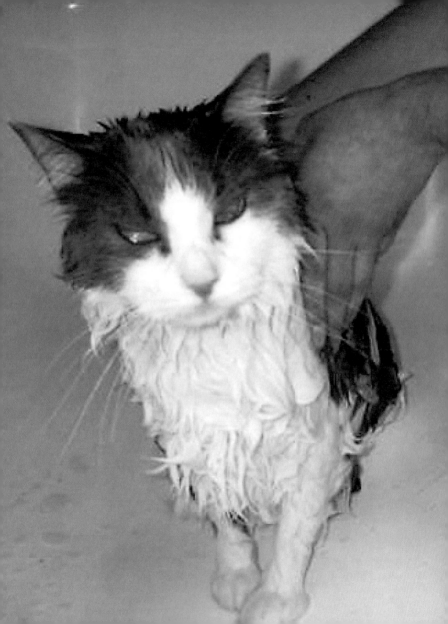

MeOwzA

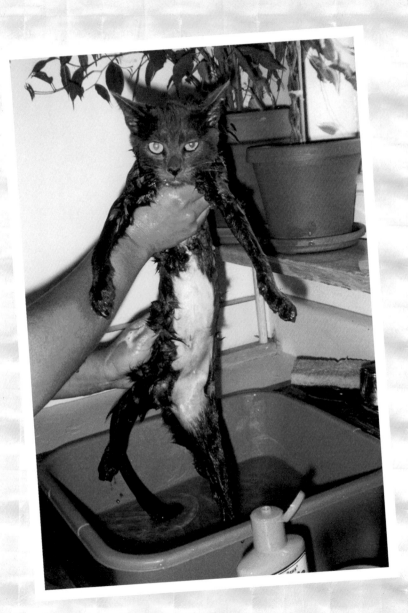

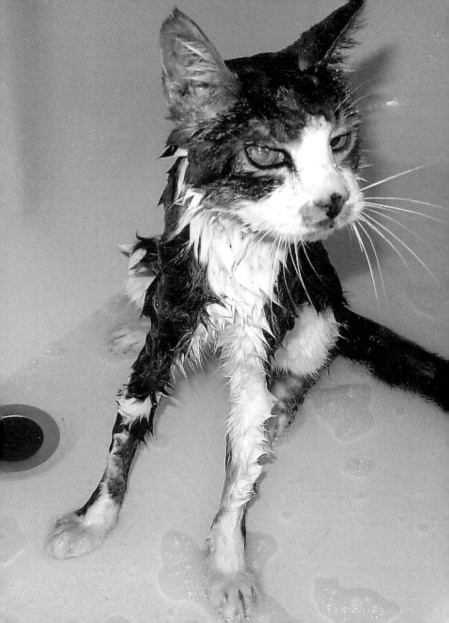

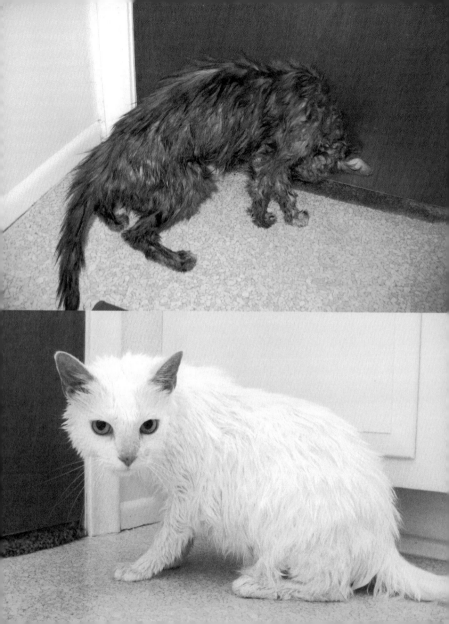

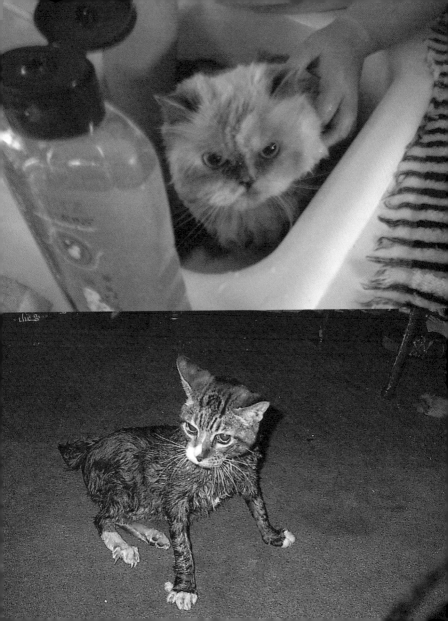

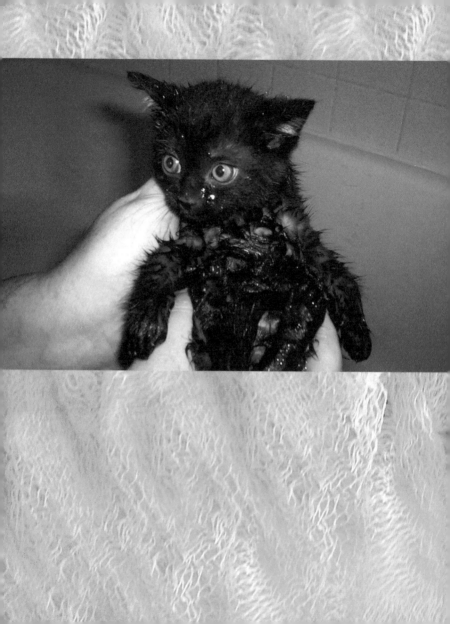

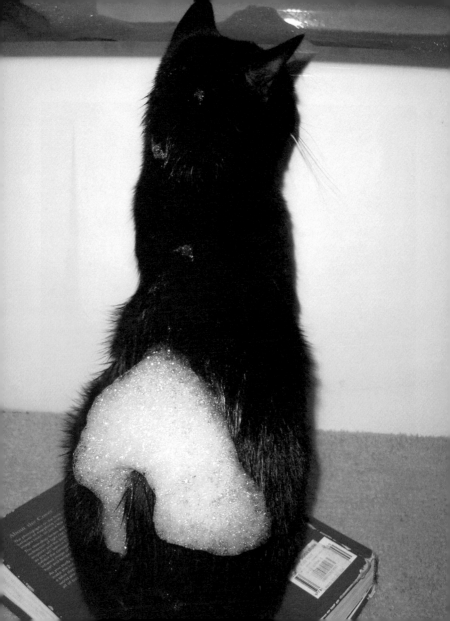

SIR GILES

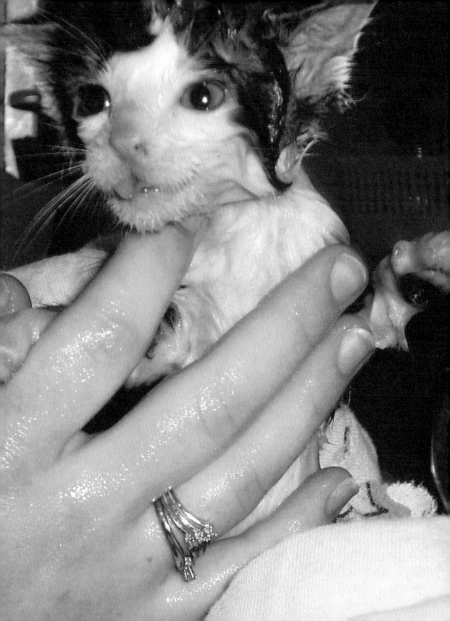

WET CAT!

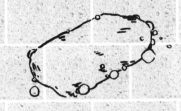

DRY CAT!

# DRY CAT!

# WET CAT!

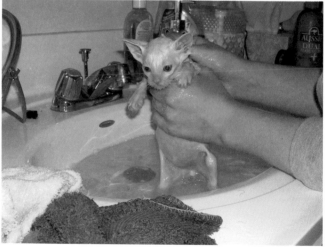

Snowflake

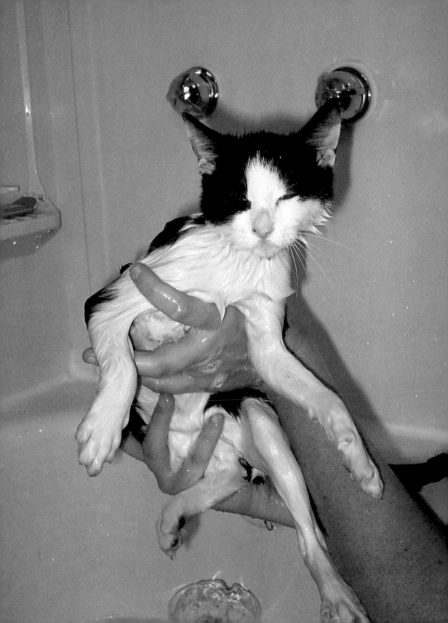

This book and the Web site would not have been possible without the help of Belinda, Brent, David, and Jason. Thanks to my friends, family, and all of the wonderful cats that have entertained me for the last two years. And thanks, too, to everyone who contributes to the site and to those I've met along the way. The stuff-on-cat revolution wouldn't be possible without the fantastic community behind it. You're the best!

**MARIO GARZA** is a graphic designer, student, and professional blogger. Inspired by the things he could stack on his cat, Love, he launched Stuffonmycat.com in the spring of 2005. Mario spends his days running an independent graphic design and screen-printing studio in Fresno, California.